James Monroe

YOUNG PATRIOT

James Monroe

YOUNG PATRIOT

by Rae Bains
illustrated by Hal Frenck

Troll Associates

Library of Congress Cataloging in Publication Data

Bains, Rae.
  James Monroe, young patriot.

    Summary: Describes the life of the fifth president
of the United States, with an emphasis on his youth
in Virginia.
    1. Monroe, James, 1758-1831—Juvenile literature.
2. Presidents—United States—Biography—Juvenile
literature. [1. Monroe, James, 1758-1831. 2. Presidents]
I. Frenck, Hal, ill. II. Title.
E372.B3   1986   973.5′4′0924 [B] [92]   85-1071
ISBN 0-8167-0557-7 (lib. bdg.)
ISBN 0-8167-0558-5 (pbk.)

James Monroe

YOUNG PATRIOT

In the 1700's, residents of the Virginia Colony
had much to be thankful for. Rich farmland
produced good crops of tobacco, vegetables, and
grains. Deep, broad forests supplied wood for
building, and game for hunters. The rivers
yielded pure, sparkling water for drinking, and
fish for the table. Opportunity, like the land
stretching westward, seemed endless.

This was the Virginia into which James Monroe was born on April 28, 1758. His parents, Spence and Elizabeth Jones Monroe, were farmers. They owned about five hundred acres of land in Westmoreland County, Virginia. The family's property was not like the grand plantations owned by some of their neighbors. Still, the Monroes were prosperous enough to be called "gentry." Gentry were people who owned land and were respected members of the community. They paid taxes, were eligible to vote, and could serve on juries.

There was great joy in the Monroe home when James was born. Four-year-old Elizabeth was especially glad to have a baby brother. It had been lonely for her, being on a farm with no other children. Now she would have someone to play with and to look after. Of course, Elizabeth could not play games with James right away, but she could rock his cradle and soothe him when he cried.

Little James did not cry too often. In fact, he was a rather quiet child. From the first, he seemed to think things through before doing anything. James was happy to play quietly, by himself or with his sister. When he was big enough to walk, James roamed freely with Elizabeth over the farm and through the surrounding woods.

Mrs. Monroe never had to worry about the children when they were out. Elizabeth and James were both sensible and cautious. They ran and climbed and stayed out for hours at a time, but never took any foolish risks. From childhood, James and Elizabeth were alike in many ways, and they remained close friends throughout their lives.

James Monroe's childhood was carefree and pleasant. His parents were loving and his world was secure. In addition to farming, Mr. Monroe earned money as a joiner, or house builder. The wages he earned as a joiner gave the family cash to pay their taxes. They also used the money to buy metal tools, gunpowder and rifles for hunting, and other manufactured goods. The Monroes did not have to buy food. They grew their own vegetables, raised chickens, geese, and pigs, and kept cows for milk, butter, and cheese.

Mr. Monroe's craft was an advantage in another way. As a joiner, he built his family a spacious, two-story home. This home was far more elegant and comfortable than houses on other properties the same size. The Monroe house was also well furnished, because Mr. Monroe made the furniture himself. There were sturdy chairs around the kitchen table, and finer spindle-backed chairs in the parlor. The

clothing chests and cabinets were smooth and
neatly fitted. They would have looked grand in
the homes of the wealthiest plantation owners.

James's mother, Elizabeth Jones Monroe,
was a sweet, sensible person. In later years,
James remembered her as "a very amiable and
respectable woman, possessing the best
domestic qualities of a good wife, and a good
parent."

In those days, a housewife like Elizabeth Monroe worked from morning till bedtime. Her chores started even before breakfast. First, she cleared the hearth of ashes and started a fresh fire. After that, the typical colonial housewife brought in water from a nearby river or stream, collected eggs from the hens' roost, and carried in food from the larder.

The larder was usually a small structure near the house, built into the ground. It was sometimes called an earth cellar, because much of it was underground. Food kept in an earth cellar stayed cool.

Why was keeping the food cool so important? There was no refrigeration in the eighteenth century. To keep food from spoiling, people dried it, salted it, stored it in a box in a cold, running stream, or in earth cellars. Even so, food spoilage was a constant problem, and people often got sick from eating bad food.

Young James and his sister also had regular chores, even as small children. When meat was roasting in the fireplace, they shared the job of turning the spit handle. At harvest time, they helped Mr. Monroe bring in the fat, ripe ears of corn, and stack the root vegetables, such as turnips, potatoes, squash, and parsnips, in the earth cellar.

There was just one job that the children really disliked: plucking goose feathers. James and Elizabeth had to pluck the geese three or four times a year. Like most colonial families, the Monroes kept geese for their down, or feathers. Only when a goose was very old was it used for food. But soft goose down was often needed for stuffing pillows, quilts, and mattresses.

In those days, houses had poor heating systems. The hearth fire gave some heat to the kitchen. But in the winter, all the rest of the house was as cold inside as it was outside. To keep warm at night, a person needed warm, goose-down bedding. But the down was not the only part of the goose people used. Colonists also sharpened the goose quills with a knife and used them as pens.

The reason children disliked plucking geese was that the geese did not like being plucked! The birds tried to bite the hands that pulled their feathers. To prevent being bitten, people covered the heads of the geese with stockings. Still, it was a messy, unpleasant job. The geese squawked, jumped around, and tried to get away. A blizzard of down flew all over, making everyone sneeze. The children were glad when a down-plucking session was over, and life returned to its normal, pleasant ways.

When James was seven years old, something happened that he never forgot. Until then, he had never heard his parents or Uncle Joseph Jones say anything against the English government. Uncle Joseph, Mrs. Monroe's brother, was a well-educated man. He was also a local judge and a deputy king's attorney for the Virginia Colony. But even *he* was angry at the British government in London.

He was angry because of a new law called the Stamp Act. Under this act, the colonists had to attach a special stamp to all legal documents and business papers. The stamps themselves were not expensive, but they had to be bought from the British government. Anyone who did not buy and use the stamps faced punishment.

The colonists objected strongly to the Stamp Act. They did not like the bother of buying and putting a stamp on every contract, newspaper, will, almanac, and many other papers, day after day. It was also the first time the British Parliament had placed a direct tax on the American colonies.

Even worse, the colonists had been given no say in the matter. British subjects, living in Great Britain, elected the members of Parliament. But the Colonies did not have anyone representing them in Parliament. It was taxation without representation, the angry colonists argued. As George Washington, then a member of the Virginia legislature, said, the Stamp Act violated the rights of America.

The events of 1765 did much to shape young James Monroe into a leading patriot in his country's cause. Even as a child, he was impressed by the strong feelings and courage shown by the protesters. First, his father and Patrick Henry put together a petition, or list of names, denouncing the Stamp Act. Then the two men took it around the countryside, encouraging others to sign it. This was a brave thing to do, as young James soon learned. It was a direct insult to the King of England, and they could be punished for it.

But Spence Monroe did not stop there. Together with other leading Virginians, he refused to buy any goods imported from England. He also would not use the stamps required by the law. This was the bravest act of all, since anyone who did not use the stamps faced a jail sentence and the anger of the authorities.

One by one, led by people like Spence Monroe, Virginians joined the protest against the Stamp Act. At the same time, there were protests in other colonies. The British government had never expected this. Their tax collectors were being beaten, chased out of towns, or simply mocked by the colonists.

These actions surprised people on both sides of the Atlantic Ocean. The British government had thought it could pass any law, and the colonists would accept it. Now they saw this was not true. Soon, the British had to back down and repeal, or cancel, the Stamp Act.

People in the Colonies suddenly had a new view of themselves. Not only could they *object* to unjust treatment, they could even win—if they stood together. Some colonial leaders, such as Ben Franklin, even suggested that King George ask the colonial assemblies to vote on taxes. That was a revolutionary idea! Imagine a king *asking* the lowest of his subjects for help! It made the colonists laugh, but it also gave them the first feelings of independence.

In the weeks that followed the protest against the Stamp Act, politics became the main subject of conversation in the Monroe house. And it stayed that way throughout James's childhood. For example, George Washington had spoken about the colonists as Americans, not British subjects, and this idea was often discussed by James's family. In fact, Spence and Elizabeth Monroe never again called themselves or their neighbors British. They were now Virginians or Americans. James, his sister, and their new baby brother, Andrew, were quick to call themselves the same.

As an adult, James Monroe felt that this early introduction to these political ideas was an important part of his education. His father brought home many of the pamphlets and newspapers read throughout the Colonies. The articles made exciting reading for young James, who did not have many books.

James did not attend school until he was eleven. Mrs. Monroe taught the children to read and write. She used whatever was available as learning tools. For example, she based the children's arithmetic lessons on the practical matters of farming and Mr. Monroe's construction business. The Monroe children added and subtracted feet and inches of lumber, multiplied numbers of bricks, and divided the corn crop by the number of rows planted. They practiced penmanship by helping their father send bills to customers. They also helped him write business letters.

Until James went to school, he did not have
any friends except his sister. Elizabeth was
often busy helping her mother, which meant
that James was alone a good deal of the time.
But being alone did not bother him, because he

always found interesting things to do. As soon as James was old enough to hold a rifle, his father taught him how to shoot and hunt. There were also chores to do, lessons to study, a horse to ride, woods to roam, and a stream in which to fish. James never complained that he was bored.

Being alone so much shaped James Monroe in other ways. He was quiet and serious throughout his life. Even when he was President of the United States, Monroe remained a modest, almost shy person. On first meeting him, people often thought he was a distant or unfriendly man. But that impression passed quickly. His warmth and liking for others soon showed themselves.

James Monroe also had the ability to make others feel at ease. He never acted as if he was more important or smarter than anyone else. Monroe also trusted people, did not expect others to be mean to him, and never was mean to others. These qualities won him the respect and admiration of everyone who knew him.

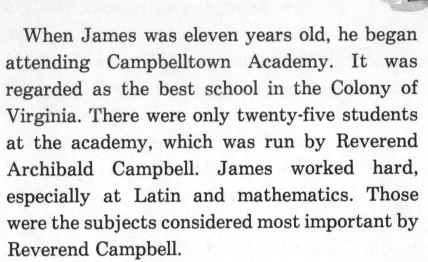

When James was eleven years old, he began attending Campbelltown Academy. It was regarded as the best school in the Colony of Virginia. There were only twenty-five students at the academy, which was run by Reverend Archibald Campbell. James worked hard, especially at Latin and mathematics. Those were the subjects considered most important by Reverend Campbell.

Young James walked to school each day, through woods and over streams. He enjoyed walking the several miles every morning and afternoon. James always carried his rifle with him, but not because of any danger. There was a good chance of spotting a rabbit, squirrel, or game bird along the way. He liked practicing his shooting and being able to bring home food.

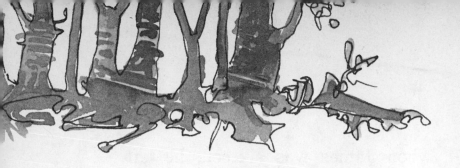

The lessons at Campbelltown Academy were hard, and James had to spend a lot of time on his studies. But he still found time for riding and swimming, fishing and hunting. Now these activities were more fun, because he had a friend who liked to do the same things. This friend was a lively, energetic boy named John Marshall.

John and James made a striking contrast. James had blue eyes and light-colored hair. John's eyes were dark brown and his hair was black. James was quiet and serious. John was a joke-teller, a prankster, and a nonstop talker. The two schoolboys got along perfectly, beginning a friendship that would last for many years. Both were patriots during the American Revolution, and both rose to high positions afterwards. John Marshall became the third Chief Justice of the Supreme Court of the United States.

In 1774, when James was sixteen, he left Campbelltown Academy. It was a turning point in his life. Mr. Monroe had just died, leaving the Monroe children orphaned. (Mrs. Monroe had died a couple of years earlier.) James's uncle, Judge Joseph Jones, was now in charge of the Monroe estate. He would continue to look after the estate until James reached the age of twenty-one.

Judge Jones felt that James had a bright future in Virginia politics. The boy was intelligent, well liked, and trustworthy. The judge was sure that with those qualities, and a good education, his nephew would succeed. The judge's plan, to which James agreed, was that the teen-ager would attend William and Mary College, to study law. James applied to the college and was accepted immediately. Although he had not had many years of schooling, he had learned a great deal in that short time.

James arrived at William and Mary late in the spring of 1774. The town of Williamsburg, Virginia, where the school was located, was bubbling with activity. In addition to the college, Williamsburg was the site of the Governor's Mansion and the House of Burgesses, the name for the colonial legislature. All those individuals involved in Virginia politics—for or against King George—were in Williamsburg. Among them were George Washington, Patrick Henry, and Thomas Jefferson.

So much was going on in the town that James and his fellow students had a difficult time keeping their minds on schoolwork. There were emotional speeches and debates every day. One of the chief topics was the trouble in Massachusetts.

In that colony, many citizens were rebelling
against English laws. For example, the British
controlled the import of tea into the Colonies,
and taxed this import heavily. In other colonies,
the people simply refused to buy British tea.
But on December 16, 1773, a number of Boston

patriots, dressed as Indians, boarded British ships at anchor and dumped 342 chests of tea into Boston Harbor. The British were furious, and passed a law called the Boston Port Bill. It closed off Boston Harbor, with the aim of starving New England into submission. The other colonies, including Virginia, sent help to Boston in the form of food, supplies, and money. The British responded by imposing harsh rules on all the colonies.

In anger, some of the Burgesses called for war. The governor of Virginia reacted to this by ordering all the Burgesses to go home. They refused, and set up their own meetings in a Williamsburg tavern. From there they sent out a call to all the colonies, to join together in a Continental Congress. The Colonies agreed to this, and arranged to meet in Philadelphia. Virginia was represented by George Washington, Richard Henry Lee, Patrick Henry, Peyton Randolph, and James's uncle, Joseph.

James Monroe managed to keep up with his studies, but his chief interests lay outside of school. With his roommate, John Mercer, James joined a group of students who drilled regularly on the campus grounds. They marched, studied military tactics, and practiced marksmanship. There was a rule against keeping guns at the school, but James and his fellow patriots ignored it.

James also took part in a surprise raid on the governor's palace, in June 1775. Of the twenty-four patriots in this group, James was the youngest. The mission was to capture the muskets, swords, pistols, and gunpowder stored in the palace. Their raid was a success, and the material they captured was later used by the Virginia militia against the British.

Throughout 1775, William and Mary students left school for military service. In January 1776, when James was seventeen years old, he enlisted in the Third Virginia Regiment. He was commissioned that summer as a lieutenant and was sent to fight in the battle of New York. There, and in later battles, he proved to be a courageous, daring, and wise officer.

The high point of James Monroe's military career came in December 1776. General Washington's weary army was camped in Pennsylvania, near the Delaware River. General Howe and his well-fed British troops were in Trenton, New Jersey, on the other side of the river. The British force far outnumbered the Americans. The British were also in better condition and better armed.

Washington felt that his best strategy was to attack, even though the odds favored the British. A surprise attack on Christmas Day was planned. First, Washington collected all the boats along a thirty-five-mile stretch of the

Delaware River. He needed the boats for his troops. Also, taking all the boats would stop the British from crossing the river to attack the Americans.

Then Washington asked for a small party of volunteers. He wanted them to cross the river ahead of the army and guard the roads leading into Trenton. The volunteers' job would be to prevent anyone from getting through to warn the British of the attack. James Monroe and one other officer volunteered to lead the fifty-soldier party.

The volunteer patrol stood guard throughout the still, icy night. Their mission was successful. When Washington's army approached Trenton at dawn, the British were caught by surprise. But the fight was just beginning. As the first Yankee gunshots rang out, a group of Hessians, (German soldiers fighting for the British) tried to set up two huge cannons. If they succeeded, the cannons would point directly at the Americans.

Lieutenant James Monroe took quick action, leading a company of troops against the Hessians. It was a bloody fight, and Monroe was seriously wounded. But the Americans drove back the Hessians and captured the cannons. General Washington praised the young lieutenant for his courage and promoted him to the rank of captain.

Captain Monroe distinguished himself as a brave soldier for the remainder of the war. Afterward, he returned to Virginia. In 1782, at the age of twenty-four, Monroe was elected to the Virginia Assembly. It was the beginning of an outstanding career as a statesman and diplomat. He served as a United States senator from Virginia, minister to France and Great Britain, and governor of Virginia.

Monroe was serving as Secretary of State, under President James Madison, when he was elected President of the United States in 1816. He served two terms as President, and during